CONFEDERATE SOLDIER
of the American
CIVIL WAR

Denis Hambucken
Matthew Payson

ACKNOWLEDGMENTS

Many thanks to the individuals and organizations that have shared
their time, knowledge, and passion with us. This book could not
have been constructed without their help.

Kermit Hummel
Chris Benedetto
Christopher Reiter
Robert Balcius
William & Ann Payson

Special thanks to members of
Co. H, 3rd Arkansas Infantry Regiment (3rd Rgt., ANV):
Scott Dyer, Tom Backus, Kris King, and Alec Franzoni

Photographs, illustrations, book design and composition by Denis Hambucken
Editing by Lisa Sacks
Historic typefaces by Walden Fonts

Library of Congress Cataloging-in-Publication Data have been applied for.
Confederate Soldier of the American Civil War
978-0-88150-977-9

Published by The Countryman Press, P.O. Box 748, Woodstock, VT 05091
Distributed by W. W. Norton & Company, Inc., 500 Fifth Avenue, New York, NY 10110

Printed in the United States of America
10 9 8 7 6 5 4 3 2 1

TO ARMS! TO ARMS!

$50 BOUNTY.

Do not wait to be Drafted, but Volunteer!!

The subscribers wish to get sixty Recruits for

CAPT. STICLEMAN'S COMPANY VIRGINIA VOLUNTEERS.

Persons wishing to enlist will find it greatly to their advantage to join this Company, as we can offer superior inducements.

You will receive pay and subsistence from the time your names are enrolled; your bounty of 50 dollars, and 25 dollars for clothing, as soon as you can be examined by an Army Surgeon.

For further particulars apply to us at Floyd Court House, Va.

LIUT. G. M. HELMS, ⎞ Recruiting
Sergt. J. W. SHELTON. ⎠ Officers

February 22, 1862.

WE WILL ATTEND THE

PUBLIC MEETINGS

to be held at the following places

Indian Valley, Saturday, March 1st: Jackson Harriss' Stillhouse, Monday, 3rd; Jacob S. Harman's Store, Friday, 7th; Oil Mills Saturday, 8th; Copper Hill, Friday, 14th; Locust Grove, Saturday, 15th, and at Floyd Court House, March, 20th (Court day.)

CONTENTS

MASTER ABRAHAM LINCOLN GETS A NEW TOY.

THE WAR BETWEEN THE STATES

THE WAR BETWEEN THE STATES

Sam Watkins, who enlisted as a private in the 1st Tennessee regiment, wrote that the common soldier of the Civil War was the one who "did the shooting and killing, the fortifying and ditching, the sweeping of the streets, the drilling, the standing guard, picket and vedette, and who drew (or was to draw) eleven dollars per month and rations, and also drew the ramrod and tore the cartridge . . ." The majority of those who fought, and who felt deeply for their part in the struggle, were average citizens: farmers and store owners, laborers and schoolteachers. They all held their own opinions of the bigger issues that faced their generation but most were more concerned with providing for and protecting their families than in joining the fiery debates ripping through statehouses and the U.S. Congress.

While slavery was at the center of the division between North and South, ultimately, it was not what motivated the majority of soldiers on either side. In his book *The Women of the South in War Times*, Matthew Page Andrews reflects the prevailing Southern sentiment when he defines the conflict as: "a struggle between an agricultural people of the South seeking free trade with the world, and a commercial and manufacturing people in the North who sought, and obtained, high protective tariffs, under which the North was able to buy cheaply the raw material of the South, while the South was compelled to pay high prices for the manufactured articles produced in the North." William M. Dame, who served as a gunner, wrote about the average soldier's motivation: "With those men it was to defend the rights of their states to control their own affairs, without dictation from anybody outside; a right not given, but guaranteed by the Constitution."

In April 1861, the Confederate attack on Fort Sumter, a Federal fort in Charleston Harbor, South Carolina, ignited the long-simmering divisions between North and South. Within a day after Union troops surrendered the fort, President Abraham Lincoln issued a call for 75,000 troops to quell the "great rebellion." Within every state, citizens were compelled to choose sides and stand for the Union or for the independence of states, with the firm belief that their own side stood for rightness and justice.

To the Union soldier of the U.S. forces, it was a fight to preserve the Republic as one nation, and to retaliate against those who had fired on the American flag at Fort Sumter. The shell-torn flag was carried through the streets of New York City like a fallen martyr, prompting thousands to answer President Lincoln's call to enlist. To the Confederate

soldier it was a fight for self-determination, the same cause for which his grandfathers had fought in the American Revolution, and to defend his home from the Federal armies that were marching south to, as President Lincoln put it, "crush the insurrection." William Fletcher, who was a private in the 5th Texas regiment, wrote that "both North and South were proving, from their viewpoint, the justness of their position by both the Bible and the Constitution, and from the preachers' views, the Lord was with us for he could prove it by the Bible; while the politician would quote some of the wording of the Constitution, and say: 'God and all civilized nations are with us.'" It was the "politician and the preacher," he felt, who had pushed the country to a point where none could see a way to resolve their grievances except in war. "And so it was blood—nothing else but blood and we surely spilled it."

From Maryland to Florida, Missouri to Texas, citizens enlisted in state defense forces, while thousands more (some even coming from Northern states) made their way to Richmond, Virginia, to defend the new Confederate capital, only 100 miles from Washington, D.C. Among them were scores of officers and soldiers of the U.S. military who returned home to serve in defense of the South, and who, along with cadets and professors from Southern military academies, helped to train and organize the thousands of new volunteers.

By July of 1861, Union armies under General MacDowell were marching south toward Richmond, Virginia. On the 21st of that month, just north of Manassas Junction, Virginia, Confederate forces under Generals Beauregard and Johnston confronted the Union Army in the first infantry battle of the war. At the end of that day, MacDowell's

FREEMEN!

OF

TENNESSEE!

The Yankee War is now being waged for "beauty and booty." They have driven us from them, and now say OUR TRADE they must and will have. To excite their hired and ruffian soldiers, they promise them our lands, and tell them our women are beautiful---that beauty is the reward of the brave.

Tennesseans! your country calls! Shall we wait until our homes are laid desolate; until sword and rape shall have visited them? NEVER! Then

TO ARMS!

and let us meet the enemy on the borders. Who so vile, so craven, as not to strike for his native land?

The undersigned propose to immediately raise an infantry company to be offered to the Governor as part of the defense of the State and of the Confederate States All those who desire to join with us in serving our common country, will report themselves immediately.

J. B. Murray.
H. C. Witt.

May 17th, 1861.

Neal & Roberts, Printers, Morristown, Tenn.

army was in full retreat to Washington, leaving several thousand dead and wounded men behind.

With such a decisive victory for the South, many felt that, for the most part, the conflict was over. To them all that remained was to serve out the rest of their twelve-month enlistments guarding the border and awaiting a settlement of peace. By the end of 1861 the conflict, though far from resolved, had come nearly to a standstill. "The war was over now," wrote Watkins, describing the common attitude as his regiment went into camp near Staunton, Virginia. "Our captains, colonels and generals were not 'hard on the boys;' in fact, had begun to electioneer a little for the Legislature and for Congress . . . whiskey was cheap, and good Virginia tobacco was plentiful, and the currency of the country was gold and silver." They spent much of their free time visiting local towns, saloons and

gambling halls. For much of the army, that fall was spent building log huts for the winter, and activity fell mostly to basic military drill, manning fortifications, and dealing with the boredom of camp life.

In 1862, all of that changed. The U.S. government in Washington had been mobilizing thousands of new troops, while reorganizing and resupplying the massive Federal armies already in the field. President Lincoln ordered an offensive on all fronts. All across the South, camps were abandoned as troops were given marching orders to meet the threats from new Federal forces. The soldiers left in "campaign trim," having quickly learned to throw away their extra clothing and camp equipment and to keep only what they could easily carry over long marches. Before long the norm for all men on campaign was to carry nothing but the bare essentials: gun and bayonet, cartridge box,

haversack, canteen, a blanket rolled up with a ground cloth (or oil cloth), and sometimes a change of underclothes. Instead of living in well-furnished camps, with tents, straw beds, cooking utensils, and extra comforts, they had to quickly adapt to life on the move, sleeping in rain or even snow, with only a thin blanket and ground cloth for cover, or the occasional lean-to of brush or tree bark. The standard ration was 1 lb. of salt pork or beef, 3/4 lbs. of bacon, and a little over 1 lb. of hardtack or cornmeal per day, but constant food shortages meant that soldiers often had to make do with half-rations or no food at all. They took to foraging for any extra food they could find, whether asking civilians or stealing from houses or farm fields, even taking haversacks from the dead. Their appearance changed as well. Hair was cropped short to make it easier to comb out lice, and many let their beards grow. Clothing became soiled to the point of decay, since there was little chance of washing on the march. When Lee's men marched into Maryland in September, 1862, one observer described them as "the dirtiest men I ever saw, a most ragged, lean and hungry set of wolves. Yet there was a dash about them that the northern men lacked." In spite of shortages of every kind, they still managed to outmarch and outfight many of their opponents. Berry Benson, of a Georgia regiment, wrote of that common bravado in the army when he described a fellow soldier that winter, "a young man, tall and vigorous, but utterly barefoot in the snow, standing in a fence corner, his gun leaning against his shoulder, and of all the proud faces I have ever seen, his was the proudest. It was a pride that seemed to scorn not only the privation and cold, but the exposure of his sufferings to others' eyes, and even the very pity it called forth."

At the first battle of Manassas, while awaiting an attacking Federal force, General Thomas "Stonewall" Jackson told his men: "When you charge, yell like furies." The wild "rebel yell" that had such a potent psychological effect on Union troops became the trademark of Confederate soldiers. The men issued hair-raising cries as they attacked, anything from the high pitched *hip he-yah* of West Texas cattlemen to the war whoop of thousands of Native Americans serving in the Confederate forces.

With the start of military campaigns in 1862, the carnage grew on a scale that was unprecedented in American history. In two days of fighting at the Battle of Shiloh in Tennessee, more than 20,000 men were wounded or killed, a grim precedent that would quickly be surpassed as the war continued to escalate. Month after month the massive armies collided all over the South, leaving in their wake tens of thousands of casualties with horrific wounds. In all, of the 1.2 million Confederate men who served throughout the war, 340,000 were killed or wounded.

In the Civil War, combat was nothing like the European tradition of troops in straight lines plodding across open fields in gentlemanly fashion – anything but. Battles were fought and won by rapid maneuvers, using the natural features of the land to shield troop movements. Attacking in large formations meant massing artillery or infantry fire on enemy positions, then deploying quickly to their front, hitting several points at once in an attempt to force their position until they were captured, killed, or routed. Rarely was it prudent to charge in the open in a solid line; rather, each regiment and brigade would move in turn almost at a run, under the covering fire of other units. At full strength an infantry regiment was made of ten companies of 100 men each, organized by state. Four or five regiments formed a brigade and several brigades formed a division, which could number up to 20,000 men.

In such massive formations, an individual soldier felt mostly insignificant. His chances of surviving depended purely on luck and happenstance, causing veteran soldiers to adopt strongly fatalistic outlooks. They were told little of the overall plan, where they were going or what to expect, and the fighting at their level was chaotic and disorienting. The men in the ranks listened for commands over the sound of artillery barrages as violent as a thunderstorm, the constant crashing of thousands of rifles, and the heavy buzzing of countless bullets cutting through the thick, acrid smoke of gunpowder and clouds of dust kicked up by thousands of feet. As Confederate private Sam Watkins wrote, in battle a soldier was "but an automaton, a machine that works by the command of a good, bad or indifferent engineer. His business is to load and shoot, stand picket, vedette, etc., while the officers sleep, or perhaps die on the field of battle and glory, and his obituary and epitaph but 'one' remembered among the slain, but to what company, regiment, brigade or corps he belongs, there is no account; he is soon forgotten."

Although consistently outnumbered in battle, at times facing twice as many well-armed and equipped Union soldiers, Confederate troops showed a dogged fighting spirit that persevered throughout the war and was attested to by many observers, including Union soldiers. Time and again they were able to hold their ground against overwhelming odds. "One thing that shone conspicuous," gunner William Dame wrote, "was the indomitable spirit of the 'Army of Northern Virginia,' their intelligence about military movements; their absolute confidence in General Lee, and their quiet, matter of course, certainty of victory, under him." As another U.S. soldier put it, "They fight like Devils."

Before 1862 was out, more than 100,000 men lay wounded in hospitals or buried in mass graves, many of them less than 30 years old. The scale of the carnage made it impossible for either side to back out. It became a war of attrition, the outcome of which, no one could yet imagine.

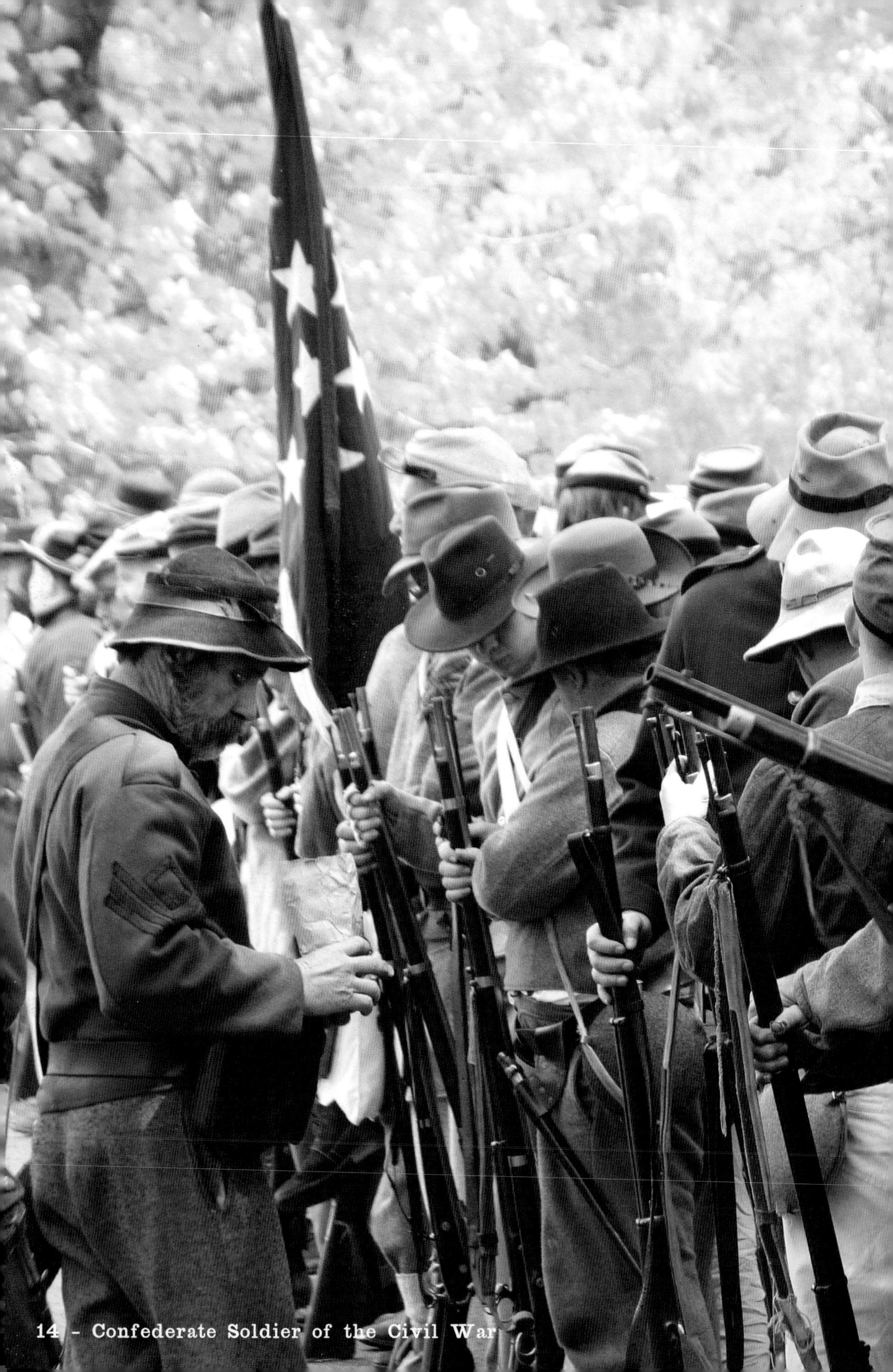

THE SOLDIER'S
DRESS & EQUIPMENT

The Soldier's Dress & Equipment

At the start of the war, equipping Confederate troops was the responsibility of individual states. As a result, appearance and equipment quality varied greatly from one regiment or brigade to another. In 1862, as the conflict escalated into an all-out war, Confederate soldiers were fairly well supplied. Most started out in regulation uniforms, including the standard frock coat, trousers, and forage cap.

1. Bayonet
2. Rifle Musket
3. Forage Cap
4. Knapsack
5. Canteen
6. Haversack
7. Bayonet Scabbard
8. Brogans
9. Blanket
10. Cartridge Box
11. Trousers
12. Frock Coat
13. Cap Pouch

Over the course of the 1862 campaigns, the Confederate soldier's dress and equipment quickly changed from the fully equipped, parade-ground soldier who resembled his Northern counterpart in many respects, to the iconic "grey-jacket rebel," an image of economy and practicality that lasted to the end of the war. Men threw away anything that might weigh them down on long marches, often carrying only a change of underclothes, a spare shirt, and socks rolled up in a blanket, along with a gun, ammunition, haversack, and canteen. The uniforms changed too, as men replaced their issue caps with slouch hats, and the newly established army depots supplied them with the more economical shell jacket, and plain, untrimmed clothing. Whatever else they might need as the fighting continued, they picked up on the battlefield.

1. Slouch Hat
2. British Enfield Rifle
3. Army-Issue Shell Jacket
4. Blanket Roll
5. Captured U.S. Canteen
6. Haversack
7. Gum Blanket
8. Cartridge Box, worn on the waist belt
9. Bayonet
10. Army-Issue Trousers
11. Captured U.S. Bayonet Scabbard

Frock Coat

The standard frock coat pattern featured colored facings denoting the branch of service: blue for the infantry, red for artillery, yellow for cavalry, and black for state militias. Almost all were made from what was known as jean cloth, a blend of roughly half wool and half cotton. Frock coats were lined with whatever wool flannel or cotton muslin fabric was available. Sometimes, they were only half lined, or not lined at all.

Great Coat

The heavy winter great coat was large enough to be worn over the uniform, with a cape attached to the collar that could be buttoned up as a hood. The ideal material was a heavy wool cloth, but great coats made in the South varied greatly in color, construction, and material. Although a great coat could be invaluable in the winter, as soon as the weather thawed in the spring, men frequently discarded the bulky garment as it became a burden on the march.

Shell Jacket

As the war dragged on, Confederate depots soon replaced the frock coats with jackets to save cost, time, and materials. Like most items produced for the Confederate armies, the jackets varied widely in pattern and material. Southern-made jean cloth was used initially, but starting in 1862 it was often replaced with supplies of grey and blue-grey uniform wool imported from Europe.

Handkerchief

The handkerchief found many uses. It was commonly tied around the neck to prevent sunburn and chaffing from the coarse jean cloth of the coat collar. It was also useful as a washcloth, and for removing a hot frying pan or tin cup from the fire.

Shirt

Undershirt

Most army-issue shirts were made from coarse materials that were too rough to be worn against the skin. Whenever possible, soldiers were issued undershirts of soft flannel, cotton muslin, or knit cotton jersey. In hot summer months a soldier might choose to wear only an undershirt beneath his coat, and at times the heat was so unbearable that men went in their shirtsleeves, often under orders to do so.

Trousers and Drawers

Most army or state-issued trousers were made of a cotton/wool blend. The fabric was durable and warmer than plain cotton, but too abrasive to be worn against the skin on long marches. For that reason, a pair of cotton drawers was usually worn underneath, even in the heat of the summer.

Mittens

Due to wool shortages Southern armies had a hard time providing their troops with proper winter clothing. Soldiers chiefly relied on mittens sent from home, scavenged from the battlefield, or improvised from whatever material was at hand. The makeshift mittens pictured above are cut from a wool blanket.

Socks

Cotton socks were commonly issued to Southern troops, but pairs of homemade wool socks sent by a wife or mother were always prized because they were ideal for long marches. Without heavy socks, a soldier's feet could become severely blistered by the rough, ill-fitting army-issue brogans.

Brogans

The common military shoe known as a "brogan" was made of rough leather, with square toes and heavy soles, lacing up over the ankle for support. Shoes wore out faster than any other article of clothing. To keep up with the demand, depots distributed almost any kind of shoes they could find, including civilian patterns and imports from England. As the war progressed, many army-issue shoes were of such poor quality (some were made with undyed leather or even rawhide) that they were barely usable. Soldiers unable to find new shoes were sometimes reduced to going barefoot, even in winter.

Battle Flags

The first flag of the Confederacy, the "stars and bars" (right), which the women of many towns across the South lovingly sewed and presented to volunteer companies leaving for the war, was based on the original U.S. flag of 1776. But in the field, it could be hard to distinguish it from the colors carried by Federal troops. A new battle flag, or guidon, was designed for army units. The field was red to be distinctive and easily visible from a distance or in low light, with a blue St. Andrew's cross in the center (based on the national flag of Scotland), lined with a star for each Confederate state. Sadly, in the 20th century, the flag became associated with bigoted groups, but to the men who originally fought under it, it was an inspirational symbol of liberty and hope.

Private Berry Benson from Georgia wrote: "Oh, how it thrilled the heart of a soldier, who had been long away from the army, to catch sight again of his red battle flag, upheld on its white staff of pine, its tatters snapping in the wind! A red rag (there be those who will say), a red rag tied to a stick, and that is all! And yet— that red rag, crossed with blue, with white stars sprinkled on the cross within, tied to a slim, barked pine sapling, with leather thongs cut from a soldier's shoe, this rough red rag my soul loved with a lover's love."

Kepi, Forage Cap, and Slouch Hats

Brimmed felt hats, often referred to as slouch hats, were invaluable. The army-issue kepis and forage caps might have looked fine on the parade ground, but they were impractical in the field, as they afforded little protection from the elements. A soldier on campaign was outdoors from morning to night in any weather. The wide brim of the slouch hat could be turned down to shade the eyes, face, and neck from the sun, as well as shed rain and snow. Soldiers purchased or commandeered any kind of brimmed hat they could find, whether the Hardee hat of a Federal soldier or a civilian specimen, sometimes going to great lengths to procure them. In mid-1862, men of the Texas brigade encamped near railroad tracks outside Richmond, Virginia, devised a highly successful method. When a train approached, the men would line up along the track, setting fires or shouting to draw attention. As the passengers stuck their heads out the windows to see what was going on, the soldiers knocked off their hats with pine boughs. Other soldiers were a bit more straightforward and simply walked up to a civilian without saying a word, plucked the hat off the man's head and walked away, leaving their old tattered hat or kepi at his feet in exchange.

Knapsack

On the march, each soldier
lived out of his pack, in which
he carried a blanket, ground cloth
(or oil cloth), spare clothing, and
personal effects. On occasion, the knapsack also held extra rations and
ammunition. With extra weight, however, it soon became uncomfortable,
putting too much strain on the shoulders. The knapsack was often one of the items
that a soldier chose to discard, preferring to carry his supplies in a blanket roll instead.

Wool Blanket

On account of wool shortages in the South during the war, blankets soon
became dreadfully thin. When supplies were short, a man might be issued a
piece of carpeting or cotton sheet instead. Some bought or pilfered any good
civilian blanket or quilt they could find, or they took blankets from dead soldiers
on the battlefield. In cold weather, blankets often doubled as overcoats. They
were tied around the shoulders, or holes were cut in the middle and they were
worn poncho-style.

Gum Blanket

The gum blankets issued to Southern troops were primarily canvas painted with linseed oil, but soldiers commonly picked up gum-rubber tarps from the knapsacks of fallen or captured Federal soldiers. The waterproof cloth, along with a wool blanket, was often the only shelter that a soldier carried. In bad weather, two soldiers would often share their bedding by laying one of their oil cloths on the ground, wrapping themselves in blankets, and covering themselves with a second oil cloth. Doing so would allow them to survive rain, snow, sleet, or severe cold when they might otherwise have frozen to death or fallen ill from exposure.

These two Confederate prisoners captured in 1863 at the battle of Gettysburg were allowed to keep some of their equipment and personal belongings on their way to a prison camp.

Blanket Roll

Soldiers routinely abandoned their bulky knapsacks in favor of the blanket roll. It was made by rolling personal items such as spare shirts, socks, and underwear into the blanket and/or gum blanket and tying the ends tightly together with a scrap of rope or twine. When the gum blanket was used, the roll was waterproof, but in bad weather soldiers sometimes preferred to keep it handy, so it could be thrown over the shoulders in heavy rain. The blanket roll was simple, lightweight, and it distributed the load comfortably across the torso.

CAMP LIFE

When on the move, the camp equipment each soldier
carried was little more than a blanket for shelter and a
canteen-half for cooking. Military operations were carried out
as late in the season as possible, but in the coldest months of
winter the weather had to be taken into account, as its effect on
soldiers could be as serious as that of enemy bullets. So the call was
usually given for troops to move into winter quarters, where they could
build shelters, wait out the cold, and enjoy a few brief weeks or months of
rest.

Once ground was chosen for an army corps, a vast perimeter was ringed
with fortified outposts and pickets guarding nearby roads and hills. The
camp was organized into sections for each regiment, and squads of
5 to 10 men worked together to build shelters. The usual structure was
little more than a lean-to, known as a Merrimac, described by Private
Berry Benson from Georgia: "two heavy forks of trees were posted in the
ground, and across the forks was laid a stout horizontal pole. Leaning
against this pole were set other poles or fence rails, the lower ends resting
on the ground. The roof thus formed was covered first with leaves, then
with earth on top of the leaves. One end was generally closed by bushes
wattled together or poles driven in the ground; the front being sometimes

left open, sometimes closed by an old blanket or oil cloth. The floor could then be covered with poles or pine boughs and beds were made by stuffing hay between two logs covered with an oil cloth.

Even in winter soldiers were kept busy. Details were constantly sent out to cut firewood, and forage parties combed the countryside for foodstuffs for the men and hay for the horses. Men were frequently required to stand shifts on guard duty, to dig fresh latrines or trenches, and to participate in military drills at least once a week. But in their free time the soldiers enjoyed their rest.

When the army in Virginia was encamped for the winter near Fredericksburg at the end of 1862, jovial snowball fights often broke out between the men. On one such occasion, the fight grew to an all-out battle as more men poured out to join in. Soon, regiments and whole divisions turned out until the whole of Longstreet's corps, officers included, were pelting each other with snowballs till the end of the day. But on the whole, the men spent their time in a more relaxed way, as gunner William M. Dame recounted, "In between our stated duties, we had some time in which we could amuse ourselves as we chose, and we had many means of entertainment. We had a chessboard, a set of quoits, dominos, and cards; and there was the highly intellectual game of 'push pin' open to all comers. Some very skillful chess players were discovered

in the company. When the weather served, we had games of ball, and other athletic games, such as foot races, jumping, boxing, wrestling, lifting heavy weights, etc. At night we would gather in congenial groups around the campfires and talk and smoke and 'swap lies,' as the boys expressed it."

In February of that winter, with the inevitable return of hostilities only weeks away, Berry Benson wrote thoughtfully in his journal, "Eat my whole day's ration at one meal. Slim, very slim. But half a loaf is better than no bread. We enjoy ourselves well for all are full of hope, conscious of our ability to cope with our enemy and look to the next thrashing we give them as the harbinger of peace."

Model 1861
Richmond Rifle Musket

The Confederate Army was equipped with a wide variety of firearms over the course of the war. At the outset of 1862, troops were armed with anything from retooled military guns, some dating back to before the American Revolution, eighty years before, to retooled hunting rifles, small batches of state-made weapons, and even the first shipments of military firearms from England, France, Belgium, and other European countries. One of the first guns to be manufactured by a Confederate state, was the Richmond Rifle Musket.

In April of 1861, when the state of Virginia voted to secede from the Union and join the Confederacy, the state quickly seized a large U.S. Army arsenal at Harpers Ferry. Among the captured stores was the production equipment for the U.S. M1855 rifle—a unique pattern gun, fitted with a Maynard tape primer that used a continuous roll of paper percussion primers (similar to modern toy gun paper cap rolls) instead of percusion caps. The machinery was quickly moved to Richmond and production began. The resulting rifles were almost exact copies of the M1855 rifle, with the exception of the lock, which was reworked to accept standard percussion caps.

More than 60,000 of these guns were manufactured, and although the imported British Enfield rifle and others were used in greater numbers, the Richmond Arsenal rifle was one of the few firearms made by the Confederacy.

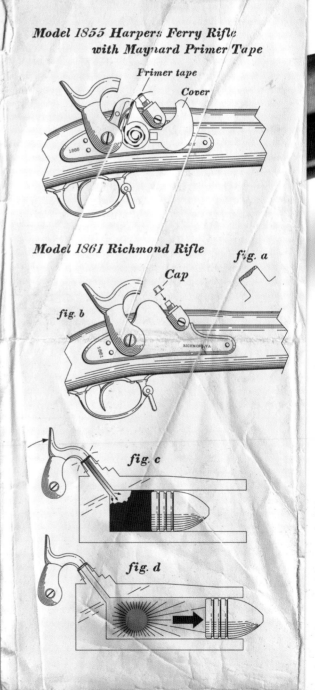

Model 1855 Harpers Ferry Rifle with Maynard Primer Tape

Primer tape

Cover

1855

Model 1861 Richmond Rifle

fig. a

Cap

fig. b

1861

RICHMOND, VA

fig. c

fig. d

Fig. a: The percussion cap is a brass or copper cap containing a small amount of mercury fulminate, an explosive compound highly sensitive to shocks.

Fig. b: The hammer is cocked and the percussion cap is fitted over the firing cone nipple.

Fig. c: When the percussion cap is struck by the hammer, the mercury fulminate detonates.

Fig. d: The detonation, communicated through the firing cone, sets off the gunpowder.

Paper Cartridges

Paper cartridges were manufactured in many cities around the South, in munitions plants known as laboratories. Confederate armies faced the logistic challenge of supplying a variety of calibers and types of guns. American .58-caliber rifles fired the highly accurate Minié ball, which had a range of up to 1,000 yards. Cartridges were distributed in packs of ten that included a tube of twelve percussion caps. The extra caps were used in case of a misfire or without a charge to clear the firing cone. To keep up with the enormous demand, the Confederacy imported large stocks of European-made ammunition. The caliber of the British Enfield rifles was such that British ammunition (above on right) could be used in .58-caliber American-made rifles as well.

Buck & Ball Cartridges

To improve the effectiveness of smoothbore muskets, many regiments were issued buck & ball cartridges. These combined the heavy stopping power of a .69-caliber lead slug with three pellets of buckshot that spread out in a wide pattern. Even a poorly aimed buck & ball shot was four times more likely to find its mark than a single bullet. Thus, one regiment supplied with buck & ball ammunition effectively had the same firepower as several.

THE MINIÉ BALL

The Civil War introduced America to a devastating new bullet that combined increased range with the loading speed of the smoothbore musket and the accuracy of the rifle. The Minié ball was named after its French inventor, Claude-Étienne Minié. Its main feature was a hollow skirt designed to expand in the barrel upon firing.

a) The undersized bullet is easily rammed down the barrel in spite of the rifling or gunpowder residue buildup.

b) The deflagration of the gunpowder flares out the skirt at the base of the bullet.

c) This produces a very tight fit against the rifling of the barrel, resulting in increased velocity and spin for longer range and improved accuracy.

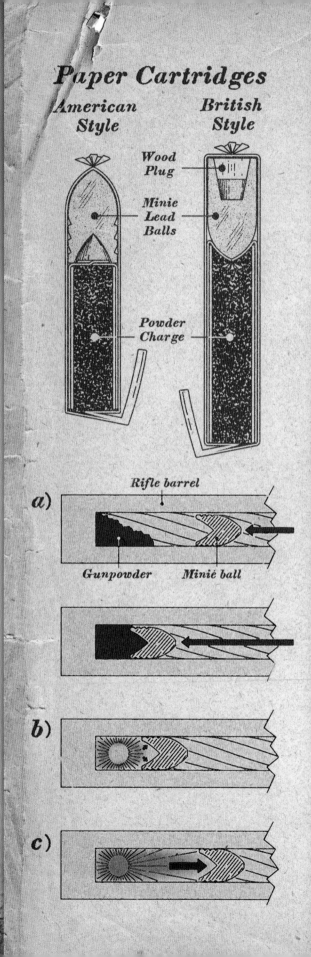

Paper Cartridges

American Style   British Style

Wood Plug

Minie Lead Balls

Powder Charge

a) Rifle barrel

Gunpowder   Minié ball

b)

c)

Cartridge Box

The standard ammunition box featured a double flap and was made of thick leather waterproofed with oil and wax – important features, as the paper cartridges could be spoiled by rain or moisture. The main compartment contained two ammunition tins. A smaller implement pouch in front typically held a musket wrench, barrel worm, cone pick, and cleaning patches for the maintenance of the musket. The cartridge box was usually carried on a 2-inch heavy leather shoulder strap. To save expense and materials however, some Southern contractors resorted to cotton webbing. Fully stocked with forty rounds of ammunition, the cartridge box weighed over 5 lbs.

10 CARTRIDGES
ENFIELD RIFLE
AND
Minnie or Rifle Musket.
CALIBRE 577 and 58.
CONICAL BALL
Charleston Arsenal, 1862

Waist Belt

Along with a cartridge box and musket, every soldier was equipped with a stout waist belt. It carried the cap pouch and bayonet scabbard, and was buckled over the shoulder strap of the cartridge box to keep it in place. Most military belts featured a decorated brass insignia buckle, but in the South, it was not uncommon to see army-issue belts fitted with the sort of plain iron utility buckles that were normally found on harnesses or baggage straps. While leather was the preferred material for belts, it was always in short supply. Army depots often resorted to cotton webbing instead.

Cap Pouch

This held a soldier's supply of percussion caps. The strip of sheepskin at the mouth of the pouch was an attempt at preventing the caps from spilling when the soldier laid prone or from bouncing out as he ran. Picking out one cap at a time quickly from the small pouch was difficult in the heat of battle. Veteran soldiers often threw away their pouches, preferring instead to keep their caps in the tool pouch of their cartridge boxes, or in their pockets.

1. A paper cartridge is retrieved from the cartridge box.

2. The cartridge is torn with the teeth. Opposable front teeth were among the few physical requirements to enlist.

3. The gunpowder is poured into the barrel, and the bullet is inserted.

4. The charge is rammed into the breech and compacted with the ramrod.

5. The hammer is pulled to half-cock, a safety position that reveals the firing cone.

6. A percussion cap is retrieved from the cap pouch.

7. The percussion cap is fitted to the firing cone.

8. The hammer is fully cocked, and the musket is ready to be fired.

Firing *the* Musket

Manuals of arms defined as many as nine distinct commands to load, aim, and discharge muskets. Although these were the object of relentless drill on parade grounds, the chaotic reality of the battlefields usually demanded a less ceremonious approach.

It was never very long before soldiers began to fire at will, either under order, or by necessity.

Musket Tools

Because gunpowder produces an abundant, sooty, and somewhat corrosive residue, a small cleaning kit was an essential part of every soldier's equipment. The musket wrench (1) was a combination wrench and screwdrivers that was used to remove the firing cone and dismantle the lock. A wire pick (2) was used to clear the firing cone, and a musket worm (3) could be screwed to the end of a ramrod to run cleaning patches (4) up and down the barrel.

Canteens

The most common type of military canteen held about a quart of water. It was made from lightweight tinned iron sheeting stamped out on presses and formed into halves that were soldered together. They were inexpensive and easily manufactured in large quantities. Many other types and styles of canteens were issued as well, including some made from wood and even leather.

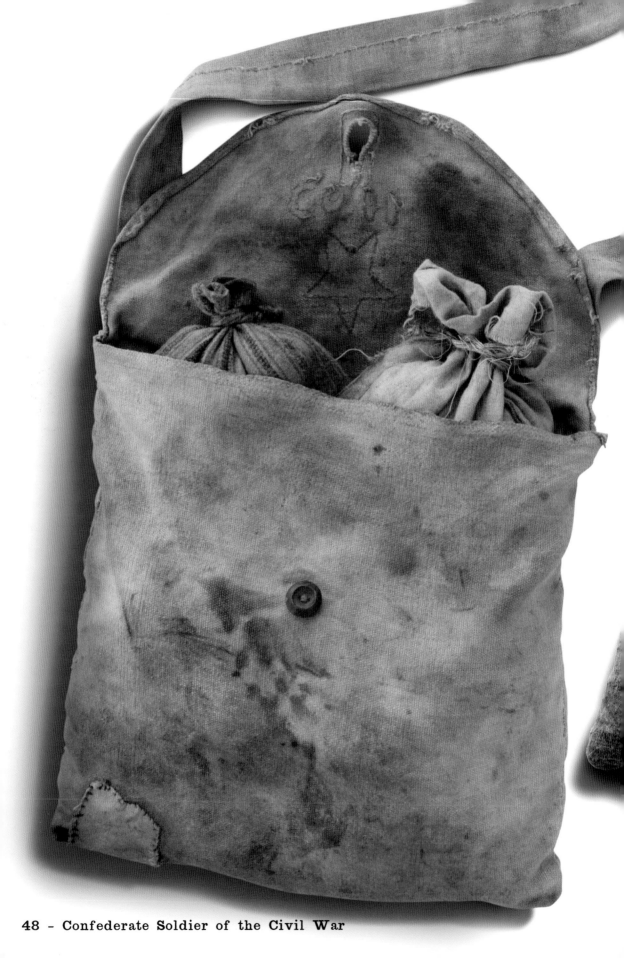

Haversack

On the march, haversacks carried several days' rations. They were usually plain, single-pocket cotton bags that could easily be washed or replaced. When not equipped with a knapsack, a soldier might also use the haversack to carry a spoon, soap, towel, or other small personal items, even a spare shirt or underclothes if there was room. The tin cup was often tied on the outside to save space.

Tin Cup

The large tin cup was often referred to as a "boiler" because it was used for boiling coffee and cooking rations. Sometimes a wire bail was attached to the cup so that it could be hung above campfires.

Coffee Substitute

Strong coffee was cherished as much as tobacco. It was warming and comforting after long marches, and it provided a much-needed boost on cold mornings. However, due to U.S. naval blockades, coffee became scarce in the South, compelling some to experiment with substitutes by roasting and grinding such ingredients as wheat and rye kernels, chicory roots, sweet potatoes, and peanuts. There are recorded instances of Union and Confederate soldiers meeting during lulls in the fighting to trade Southern tobacco for Northern coffee.

Mess Kit

Aside from the tin cup, eating utensils were usually limited to a tin plate, spoon, and pocketknife. The lightweight tin plate was also used to mix a dough of cornmeal or flour, or as a frying pan.

Beans and Peas

Dried peas and beans were staple ration foods because they were easily preserved. Other dried vegetables, and sometimes dried peaches or apples, were also issued on occasion. When boiled with meat, rice, or other rations in a stew, they provided vitamins that the typical army ration of meat and bread lacked. Without a regular source of vegetables, soldiers suffered from illnesses such as scurvy, caused by a severe deficiency in vitamin C.

Hardtack

Flour- or corn-based, brick-hard crackers could be stored almost indefinitely. They were sometimes jokingly referred to as "tooth dullers" or "sheet iron." The preferred way to prepare them was to soften them in water then fry them in bacon grease, but on the march, soldiers often ate them "raw" with a piece of salt pork, bacon, or some sugar.

Pocketknife

A spoon and a pocketknife were often the only utensils a soldier needed. Since most soldiers lived outdoors year round, a good knife found hundreds of other uses. Many soldiers took to wood carving, using their pocketknives to whittle ornate smoking pipes, or "Kentucky buttons," toggle buttons made from pieces of stick.

Smoked Bacon

Compared to our modern version, 19th-century bacon was much more heavily salted and smoked. Thus cured, it could last several months without refrigeration. When sliced and cooked in a pan, it released a lot of fat that was used to fry and flavor hardtack, flour biscuits, or cornmeal rations that would otherwise have been flavorless and almost inedible.

Sugar

Used to sweeten coffee or added to ration foods for flavor, sugar (when available) was a delicacy to the often poorly fed Southern troops. Brown "molasses" sugar was the most common type, but due to shortages in the South, it was sometimes substituted with sorghum syrup.

Cornmeal

Grits or cornmeal were more frequently issued to Southern troops than hardtack or bread. They were mixed with water and boiled in a tin cup until soft, then mixed with flour to form a dough. The dough was usually pressed into cakes and baked on a heated rock near the fire, or fried in bacon fat.

"Coosh" Recipe

Fry bacon till the pan is half full of hot grease. Mix flour with water until it flows like milk. Pour the mixture into the hot grease and stir rapidly till the whole is a dirty brown mixture with the consistency of thick gravy. The coosh is now ready to be served. You can use boiled grits or cornmeal instead of flour and add bits of bacon, pork, onion, or other vegetables. Fry it all together into a mash.

Coosh and countless variations soon became favorites of soldiers on the march. Coosh was easy and quick to make, tasty, and filling.

Writing Kit

As early as 1861, the Confederate government established a national postal system that reached every state and functioned effectively throughout the war, keeping letters and care packages from home going out to the troops in the field. To keep up correspondence and journals, some soldiers brought along writing kits such as this one, complete with paper, envelopes, pens, pencils, and other items. Most of these kits were discarded as the war went on, many preferring to keep only a pencil or small pen and an ink bottle rather than carry the weight of a full kit.

Toiletries

On campaign, very little was carried for personal hygiene, though many men held on to a few toiletries such as a toothbrush, scissors or razor, a hand towel, and sometimes a comb. Soap was issued rarely, and then usually in small amounts. Thousands of troops marching on dirt roads in the summer would kick up immense clouds of dust that covered each soldier from head to toe. Numerous accounts of Southern troops mention how they often stuck their toothbrushes in a buttonhole of their jackets or in the band of their hats so as to easily brush the dust from their teeth. William Dame, of the Richmond Howitzers, described a routine "campaign wash" when water or a stream was not available. "One fellow poured a little water, out of the canteen, into his comrade's hands, with which he moistened his face and neck, a little more was poured over his soaped hands, and the deed was done . . . when one canteen had to serve for three, and no more water was to be had . . . it was little more than a pantomime."

Sewing Kit

Soldiers had to mend their clothing to make it last, since new uniforms were only issued a few times a year at best. The makeshift kit shown here includes thread, a few sewing needles, a nail sharpened into a leather awl, a piece of candle to wax the thread, and buttons and patches saved from discarded clothing. William Dame recalled how sometimes the men had a bit of fun by making blatantly showy patches. One man in his unit covered the holes in the seat of his pants with, "A large patch in the shape of a heart transfixed with an arrow, done out of red flannel," soon, others did the same, and "Upon the seats were displayed figures of birds, beasts and men, a spread eagle, a cow, a horse, a cannon . . ." This particular kit also includes a couple of fish hooks and a bobber. There are many accounts of men in quiet sectors fishing to pass time and supplement their rations. When the Army of Northern Virginia camped near Fredericksburg in the winter of 1862, fishing details were regularly sent out to the Rappahannock to catch as many fish as possible.

Tobacco

The "flower of the South," tobacco was one of the few luxuries that the Confederate soldier could enjoy on a regular basis. It was such an abundant crop in Southern states that it was sometimes issued with rations, mostly in the form of plug tobacco, chewing tobacco mixed with molasses and pressed into small bricks. Smoking tobacco for pipes could be purchased from sutlers or local farmers. Many high-ranking officers were known to keep a supply of the more upscale cigars with them at all times.

Pocket Watch

Nineteenth-century watches ran on metal springs that had to be wound daily with small keys. Expensive watches were made from solid gold or silver, while cheaper versions such as this one were made of coin silver or pewter. Officers relied heavily on pocket watches to see that troop formations, guard details, and other military duties were preformed precisely on schedule.

Matches

Friction matches were a relatively recent invention that still presented serious hazards. They were formulated with highly toxic white phosphorus that could cause "phossy jaw," a painful, disfiguring disease. Matches were sensitive enough to be struck on any rough surface. So sensitive indeed that it was dangerous to carry loose matches in a pocket or bag for even a slight friction or shock was sometimes enough to set them off. To keep matches dry, and to reduce the risk of injury, people usually carried them in small metal boxes, known as "match safes."

Currency

Although 1861 saw the first attempts at minting Confederate coins, for lack of metal, paper currency from Richmond became the standard early in the war. However, these paper bills were promissory notes guaranteeing payment "six months after the ratification of a treaty of peace with the United States of America." As the odds of a victory waned and the value of the Confederate bills plummeted, many Southerners preferred to place their faith in U.S. coins, as illustrated here. Even if he was lucky enough to be paid in coins, a soldier's wage was only $11 per month; less than half the average salary before the war.

Photographs

It was common practice when separated from one's family to bring along locks of hair as comforting mementos. This practice endured even as the emerging technology of wet collodion photography made it possible for homesick soldiers to carry the likenesses of their loved ones.

WOMEN AND THE WAR

Many women and civilian men were just as involved in supporting the war effort as those serving in the army. Phoebe Yates Pember, a superintendent at a Richmond military hospital, wrote: "The women of the South had been openly and violently rebellious from the moment they thought their states' rights touched. They incited the men to struggle in support of their views, and whether right or wrong, sustained them nobly to the end. They were the first to rebel—the last to succumb."

Women helped turn the mostly unprepared, underdeveloped South into an organized nation, running factories and producing raw materials to keep the country and the armies in motion. Every effort was made to donate food, clothes, and dry goods for the troops at the front. To fight chronic shortages, they improvised various substitutes for everything from salt to candles, and clothing.

Women, even girls as young as nine years old, worked in factories, including laboratories where rifle cartridges and other munitions were prepared. It was extremely dangerous work, and despite all safety precautions, accidents occurred. The worst was in 1863, when an explosion at a munitions plant on Brown's Island in Richmond killed more than 50 young women and grievously wounded many others. Still, the necessary factory work continued throughout the war.

Women also made major contributions in hospitals. Early on, in an effort to free up military personnel for the front, Congress called for women across the South to serve as nurses and administrators, positions that had been exclusively held by men up to

This etching, published in the September 6, 1862, issue of Harper's Weekly, pays tribute to the contribution of women to the war effort, preparing ammunition, knitting and sewing clothing for the troops, doing camp laundry, and writing letters on behalf of wounded soldiers.

that point. Initially, many doctors felt that a military hospital was no place for women, but before long, women proved themselves competent nurses and aids, serving meals to thousands of patients even when food supplies were disastrously low, administering drugs, and also organizing and running wards, assisting in medical procedures, and comforting the convalescent and the dying. It was largely their work during the Civil War that opened to medical professions to women and paved the way for women nurses and doctors in the generations that followed.

Harmonica

Music and songs, performed by
regimental bands or less formally on the march
or around campfires, were a favorite source of entertainment
and a morale booster. The most popular songs of the time included "Dixie,"
"Maryland, My Maryland," and "The Bonnie Blue Flag."

Playing Cards and Dice

Gambling was officially banned in army camps, but the rule was seldom enforced, and even officers took part in the games. It was one of very few ways to pass time and relieve tension. Professional cardsharps often set up tents near military camps to cheat soldiers out of their money. In the winter of 1862, one spot near Fredericksburg was known as "the devil's half-acre" as it was teeming with purveyors of every kind of debauchery. They camped in the woods by day and plied their trade to venturing soldiers by night.

Liquor

Whiskey was at times rationed out to the men as a reward or a stimulant before battles or during long marches. But there were strict penalties against drunkenness on duty, and in general, enlisted men were not allowed to keep supplies of liquor. That, however, never stopped them from seeking out wine, brandy, whiskey, or any other type of alcohol that could easily be procured when they passed through towns.

Hazard

Hazard was a popular game, played with two dice and any number of players.

The first player, or caster, calls a number between 5 and 9, puts down a wager, and tries to roll his number with the dice. The other players bet against the caster, matching or raising the wager.

The dice are rolled. If they add up to the number called out, the caster wins the bet.

If the dice add up to 2 or 3, the caster loses and the other players collect.

If the dice fall on any other number (4, 10, 11, or 12), the caster rolls the dice again and tries for the number he called.

The caster holds on to the dice until he loses 3 times, at which time he passes the dice to the player to his left.

THE UNION SOLDIER

THE UNION SOLDIER

By the end of the Civil War, more than 2 million men had served as volunteers or conscripts in the Union Armies between 1861 and 1865. The vast majority of volunteers at the beginning of the war had little or no familiarity with warfare and military protocol, but most shared a desire to save the Union, earn glory on the battlefield, and of course, collect the enlistment bounty. A large proportion of them were recent immigrants from Ireland or Germany who came to work in the mills of New England or to start a new life in the fertile farmland of Pennsylvania and the Midwest. Beginning in 1863, the Union armies received a significant boost from nearly 200,000 African American men, many of them former slaves, who were eager to fight and prove their worth as loyal and capable soldiers.

No matter where he was from, if a volunteer was deemed eligible for military service after a brief physical examination, and most were, he signed a state enlistment form that included his age (he lied if he needed to circumvent age requirements), place of birth, occupation, and a basic physical description. New recruits reported to training camps that were buzzing with activity as officers attempted to turn civilians into disciplined soldiers. Before leaving their home states, regiments were mustered into Federal service and presented with battle flags that would be

hoisted on battlefields from Pennsylvania to Louisiana and beyond.

The infantry regiment, which on paper totaled about 1,000 men split into ten companies, was the single most important unit in the Union armies. Like their Southern foes, the quality and morale of Union regiments largely depended on the competence and character of their officers and noncommissioned officers. Some units were poorly drilled and ineffective in battle because their officers had received their commissions through political connections rather than military prowess, but many volunteer regiments in the Union Army became legendary for their stamina under grueling conditions and their effectiveness under fire. The typical chain of command in a company included eight corporals and five sergeants who received their orders from lieutenants and a captain. These officers ultimately reported to the colonel. Other commissioned officers in a typical regiment included a surgeon, and a quartermaster charged with issuing uniforms, equipment, and rations to the men.

But disease and combat took a heavy toll and by 1863, the average size of a "fighting" regiment was no more than three to four hundred men. As the war dragged on for four bloody years, the demographic of the Union Army inevitably changed. The number of volunteers dropped steadily as the brutality of the war became evident. States and communities offered bounties totaling hundreds of dollars to encourage civilians to enlist. During the summer of 1863, the Federal government also instituted its first draft (the Confederacy had already done so in April 1862), which resulted in violent riots in cities across the North. The familiar phrase "rich man's war, poor man's fight" was coined because affluent men who were drafted could pay $300 for a substitute to take their place. Not surprisingly, conscripts were disdained by other Union soldiers who had voluntarily put themselves in harm's way.

In the Union armies, four or five regiments were typically grouped into a brigade; there were three brigades in a division, and three to four divisions typically made up an army corps totaling up to 20,000 men. To equip, feed, and supply armies of this magnitude was a task far beyond the capacity of the existing Federal arsenals. The Union Government imported some weapons and gear, including the Enfield rifle from England, but mostly, it contracted with privately owned mills and factories to produce millions of largely standardized uniforms, shoes, accouterments, weapons, and ammunition.

In the end, the Confederacy was overwhelmed not only by the industrial war machine of the North and the massive size of its armies, but also by the Union soldiers' determination to preserve the United States.

The Union Soldier's Dress & Equipment

As Carlton McCarthy of the Richmond Howitzers put it, "The arms and ammunition of the Federal soldiers were abundant and good,— so abundant and so good that they supplied both armies, and were greatly preferred by Confederate Officers."

Northern states were much more industrialized than the South, and their factories, farms, and railroads were safe from the fighting. As a result, Federal troops were much better supplied and their appearance remained more consistent throughout the war. In sharp contrast, the Confederate Army, facing shortages of every kind, came to rely heavily on Union equipment scavenged from battlefields.

1. Forage Cap
2. Springfield Rifle Musket
3. Blanket
4. Knapsack
5. Cartridge Box
6. Canteen
7. Haversack
8. Cup
9. Bayonet Scabbard
10. Trousers
11. Brogans
12. Corporal Stripes
13. Issue Coat
14. Belt Plate
15. Waist Belt
16. Bayonet
17. Cap Pouch

Index

FOR FURTHER READING:

Denis Hambucken, Chris Benedetto. *Union Soldier of the American Civil War* (Woodstock, VT: Countryman Press, 2012)

Wiley, Bell Irvin. *The Life of Johnny Reb* (Baton Rouge: Louisiana State University Press, 1943)

McPherson, James M. *For Cause and Comrades: Why Men Fought in the Civil War* (New York: Oxford University Press, 1997), 96-97.

Barrow, Charles Kelly, and Joe Henry Segars. *Black Southerners in Confederate Armies: A Collection of Historical Accounts* (Gretna, LA: Pelican Publishing, 2007)

Abel, Annie Heloise. *The American Indian as Participant in the Civil War* (Project Gutenberg, 2004) www.gutenberg.org/files/12541/12541-h/12541-h.htm.

Watkins, Sam R. *Company Aytch: Or, a Side Show of the Big Show and Other Sketches* (Wilmington, NC: Broadfoot Publishing Co., 1994)

Andrews, Matthew Page. *The Women of the South in War Times* (The Norman, Remington Co., 1920)

McCarthy, Carlton. *Detailed Minutiae of Soldier Life in the Army of Northern Virginia, 1861–1865* (Project Gutenberg, 2008) www.gutenberg.org/files/25603/25603-h/25603-h.htm.

Dame, William Meade. *From the Rapidan to Richmond and the Spottsylvania Campaign* (Baltimore: Green-Lucas Co., 1920)

Fletcher, W. A. *Rebel Private Front and Rear* (Reprint. Meridian, 1997)

Thomas, Emory M. *Robert E. Lee: a biography* (W. W. Norton & Company, 1997)

Benson, Susan Williams, ed. *Berry Benson's Civil War Book* (Athens, Georgia: University of Georgia Press, 1992)

Williamson, M. L., ed. McHugh, Michael J. *The Life of General Stonewall Jackson* (Arlington Heights, IL: Christian Liberty Press, 1989)

Pember, Phoebe Yates. Bell Irvin Wiley, ed. *A Southern woman's story: life in Confederate Richmond: including unpublished letters written from the Chimborazo Hospital* (Reprint. Mockingbird Books, 1974.)